Congressional
Research
Service

Photo ID Requirements for Voting: Background and Legal Issues

Kevin J. Coleman
Analyst in Elections

Eric A. Fischer
Senior Specialist in Science and Technology

L. Paige Whitaker
Legislative Attorney

November 2, 2012

Congressional Research Service

7-5700

www.crs.gov

R42806

Summary

Some states require voters at a polling place to produce photographic identification (photo ID) before casting a ballot. Such requirements have emerged as a controversial issue in the 2012 presidential election, and they are the focus of this report.

Since 2008, almost half the states have enacted laws, many in 2012, relating to voter identification, with several containing photo ID requirements. In contrast, while several bills with voter identification provisions have been introduced in the 112th Congress, none have received committee or floor consideration.

About 30 states require voters to provide some form of identification when voting in person, although few require such documentation for absentee voters. Seven of these states require a photo ID for polling-place voting but permit alternatives such as signing an affidavit for voters without an ID. With respect to what type of photo ID is acceptable and what happens if a voter does not have it, no two states are the same.

Four states—Georgia, Indiana, Kansas, and Tennessee—permit only voters who present a photo ID to cast a ballot, with few exceptions. Pennsylvania, South Carolina, Texas, and Wisconsin recently enacted similarly strict photo ID requirements that are not in effect at present because of court or U.S. Department of Justice (DOJ) actions.

In 2008, the U.S. Supreme Court upheld the Indiana voter photo ID law under the U.S. Constitution on equal protection grounds. However, in more recent cases, the question being considered is whether such laws violate relevant *state* constitutions. For example, a Pennsylvania court recently issued a preliminary injunction to a portion of a new state law, predicting that implementation for the November 6, 2012, election would result in voter disenfranchisement. As a result, election officials in Pennsylvania will be permitted to ask voters for the requisite ID, but will be required to accept and count the ballots of qualified voters who do not present ID, and such voters will not be required to cast provisional ballots.

Whether voter photo ID laws comport with the Voting Rights Act (VRA) has also recently been considered by the courts and DOJ. Section 5 of the VRA requires certain states and jurisdictions to obtain preclearance from either DOJ or the U.S. District Court for the District of Columbia before implementing a change to any voting practice or procedure. For example, in March 2012, DOJ denied preclearance approval under Section 5 to laws in Texas and South Carolina that require voters to show photo ID prior to casting a ballot. Subsequently, federal courts also denied preclearance to both laws, so they will not be in effect for the November 6, 2012, election. The South Carolina law, however, was granted preclearance to take effect in any election beginning in 2013. Photo ID requirements enacted in Alabama and Mississippi are slated for implementation after 2012, and are also subject to preclearance.

Supporters of photo ID requirements emphasize the need to prevent voter fraud, while opponents emphasize the need to avoid disenfranchising legitimate voters who do not have ready access to a photo ID. Polling data suggest that most voters and most local election officials support a photo ID requirement but that many are also concerned about the risk of disenfranchisement. The policy controversy centers largely on whether the risk of disenfranchisement or the risk of voter fraud is the greater threat to the integrity of the electoral process. This policy debate is being conducted in the absence of a broad consensus about the evidence pertaining to those risks.

Election administration is complex, and changes in photo ID requirements may affect other aspects as well, among them the use of provisional ballots, the potential for long lines, and the possibility that poll workers could misapply the new rules. It may be advantageous to have as much time as possible to implement changes to voting procedures, so that election officials, poll workers, and voters have time to adjust. The new photo ID procedures in effect for 2012 may provide a test of that view.

Contents

Tables

Contacts

Introduction and Overview

More than half the states require a voter to provide a form of identification (ID) to cast a ballot and some of those states require a specified form of photographic identification (photo ID) in order to vote. Seventeen states and the District of Columbia do not require any type of identification document to vote, but a voter may be asked to provide certain information to verify what is contained in the registration record or otherwise confirm his or her identity, such as stating an address or birth date or providing a signature. Washington and Oregon conduct elections entirely by mail. Since 2006, states have been required under the Help America Vote Act (HAVA, P.L. 107-252) to maintain a single, computerized list of all registered voters that every election official in the state can access.[1]

Identification requirements across the states vary in flexibility, in the type of documents allowed, in exceptions made to the requirements, and in the recourse available to a voter who cannot comply with the ID requirement at the polls. This report provides an overview of a particular type of identification—photo ID. A full accounting of all identification requirements is beyond the scope of this report. The report discusses the origins of photo ID, federal legislative action in the 112th Congress related to voter identification, and background and legal issues related to photo ID laws in the states.

Current Status of Photo ID in the States

Among those states that require voters to show an identification document for the November 2012 election, four permit only photo IDs (Georgia, Indiana, Kansas, and Tennessee) while others permit other means of identification for voters without photo IDs (see **Table 1**).[2] In addition, South Carolina, Texas, and Wisconsin recently enacted photo ID requirements that are not in effect at present because of court or U.S. Department of Justice (DOJ) action (discussed in detail in the section of this report entitled "Legal and Constitutional Issues Regarding Voter Photo Identification Laws"). As a result of a court order issued on October 2, 2012, Pennsylvania election officials may ask for, but not require, photo ID to cast a ballot in the November 2012 election (see "Constitutionality of Voter Photo ID Laws" below). Mississippi voters approved a constitutional amendment in 2011 to require a photo ID for voting,[3] but it will require

---

[1] §303. Under the requirement states must maintain a "single, uniform, official, centralized, interactive computerized statewide voter registration list" that contains the name and registration information of every registered voter in the state and to which every election official, including local officials, may obtain "immediate electronic access to the information contained in the computerized list." The requirement does not apply to states that do not have voter registration (North Dakota). Voters in North Dakota must provide an acceptable ID (driver's license; passport; tribal, military, or student ID; a current utility bill; or a USPS verification of a change of address form) or be vouched for by a pollworker in order to vote.

[2] Interpretation of the requirement may not always be clear-cut. For example, the Kansas requirement does not include an alternative to photo ID for most voters, but it exempts some voters with disabilities, members of the military, and people with religious objections to being photographed. New Mexico requires an ID document, but permits voters who do not have one to vote a regular ballot if they correctly state name, registration address, and year of birth.

[3] The initiative as approved by voters would require a government issued photo ID to vote, would provide free photo ID to any voter who lacked one, and would exempt certain residents of state-licensed care facilities and those with a religious objection from the requirement to show photo ID. The initiative language may be found at, http://www.sos.ms.gov/page.aspx?s=7&s1=1&s2=84.

---

implementing legislation or administrative rules to take effect, according to the National Conference of State Legislatures,[4] and must be precleared by the Department of Justice. Alabama voters would be required to provide photo ID beginning in 2014, with that law also requiring DOJ preclearance.

The Help America Vote Act Identification Requirement and the Origins of Photo ID

A number of developments during the past 12 years may have focused attention on identification requirements for voting. After the 2000 election, numerous studies and reports were issued that assessed the nation's voting process, or aspects of it, and made policy recommendations. Perhaps the best known study was issued in August 2001 by the National Commission on Federal Election Reform, sponsored by the Miller Center of Public Affairs at the University of Virginia and The Century Foundation and co-chaired by Presidents Gerald R. Ford and Jimmy Carter (often referred to as the "Carter-Ford Commission").[5] The report noted that states should work to improve "verification of voter identification at the polling place"[6] and recommended that they

> require those who are registering to vote and those who are casting their ballot to provide some form of official identification, such as a photo ID issued by a government agency (e.g., a driver's license). A photo ID is already required in many other transactions, such as check-cashing and using airline tickets. These Commissioners point out that those who register and vote should expect to identify themselves. If they do not have photo identification then they should be issued such cards from the government or have available alternative forms of official ID. They believe this burden is reasonable, that voters will understand it, and that most democratic nations recognize this act as a valid means of protecting the sanctity of the franchise.[7]

Many of the report's recommendations were incorporated in the Help America Vote Act (HAVA) when it was enacted a little more than a year later in 2002, including a limited voter identification requirement. HAVA requires that an individual who registers to vote by mail and has not previously voted in a federal election in the jurisdiction provide a current, valid photo ID *or* a copy of a current utility bill, bank statement, government check, paycheck, or other government document with the voter's name and address, whether voting in person or by mail.[8] The requirement does not apply to a voter who registers under the National Voter Registration Act of 1993 (P.L. 103-31) and submits with the registration application one of the required identifications or who provides a driver's license number or the last four digits of the voter's Social Security number that matches an existing state record with the same number, name, and date of birth as provided in the registration. A voter who does not provide one of the required documents may vote a provisional ballot that is counted in accordance with state law if the appropriate election official determines that the voter is eligible.

---

[4] See the discussion of Mississippi's ID requirement in Table 2, titled, "Details of Voter Identification Requirements," at http://www.ncsl.org/legislatures-elections/elections/voter-id.aspx.

[5] The National Commission on Federal Election Reform, *To Assure Pride and Confidence in the Electoral Process*, August 2001, at http://web1.millercenter.org/commissions/comm_2001.pdf.

[6] Ibid, p. 14.

[7] Ibid, p. 31.

[8] §303 (b).

Following passage of HAVA, states enacted laws to implement the HAVA identification requirement, and in some cases, more stringent requirements. A related provision of HAVA made clear that states were free to adopt stricter election administration requirements than those imposed by HAVA:

> The requirements established by this title are minimum requirements and nothing in this title shall be construed to prevent a State from establishing election technology and administration requirements that are more strict than the requirements established under this title so long as such State requirements are not inconsistent with the Federal requirements under this title or any law described in section 906.[9]

Another related development was the passage of legislation in the House of Representatives in the 109th Congress to require photo ID and proof of citizenship to vote. The Committee on House Administration reported an amended version of H.R. 4844 (Hyde) on September 14, 2006, which was taken up and passed by the House on September 20.[10] It was not taken up by the Senate before the 109th Congress adjourned. The amended version of the bill would have required a government issued photo identification (beginning in 2008) and proof of citizenship (beginning in 2010) for voting in federal elections. It would have required that voters who cast a provisional ballot because they did not have the required identification provide such within 48 hours for the ballot to be counted. It included an exception for military and overseas voters. The bill would have required states to provide photo ID documents to qualified voters who did not have such documents, and to provide them to indigent voters at no cost. It would have authorized appropriations to cover the costs of providing such identification to indigent voters.

Public Opinion

Public opinion surveys over time have tended to show significant majority support for requiring photo ID to vote. A Pew Research Center poll from October 2006 found that 78% of respondents answered yes when asked whether voters should be required to show photo ID; 18% answered no.[11] A similar Pew Research Center poll from October 2012 found that 77% of respondents believed that voters should be required to show "official photo ID before they vote on election day," while 20% did not. When asked whether they had the "identification you might need to vote?" 98% answered yes, 1% said no, and 1% volunteered that identification was not needed.[12]

A *Washington Post* poll from August 2012 asked a series of questions about photo ID and vote fraud, and found that 74% or respondents believed that voters should be required to show "official, government-issued photo identification, such as a driver's license" to vote, while 23% did not.[13] In response to a question that asked whether voter fraud is a major problem, minor

---

[9] §304. The statutes referred to in §906 are the Voting Rights Act of 1965, the Voting Accessibility for the Elderly and Handicapped Act, the Uniformed and Overseas Citizens Absentee Voting Act, the National Voter Registration Act of 1993, the Americans with Disabilities Act of 1990, and the Rehabilitation Act of 1973.

[10] The vote was 228-196 in favor of the bill.

[11] Pew Research Center for the People & the Press, "Democrats Hold Double-Digit Lead in Competitive Districts," October 26, 2006, at http://www.people-press.org/2006/10/26/democrats-hold-double-digit-lead-in-competitive-districts/.

[12] Pew Research Center for the People & the Press, "Broad Support for Photo ID Voting Requirements," October 11, 2012, at http://www.people-press.org/2012/10/11/broad-support-for-photo-id-voting-requirements/.

[13] Washington Post Poll, "Fear of Voter Suppression High, Fear of Voter Fraud Higher," August 13, 2012, at http://www.washingtonpost.com/politics/polling/voter-identification-laws-washington-post-poll/2012/08/13/13829cb0-(continued...)

problem, or not a problem in presidential elections, 48% believed it is a major problem, 33% considered it a minor problem, and 14% believed vote fraud is not a problem. Another question asked whether voter suppression—described as eligible voters taken off registration lists or denied the right to vote—is a major problem, minor problem, or not a problem in presidential elections; 41% believed it is a major problem, 32% believed it is a minor problem, and 20% believed it is not a problem. One question joined those two concepts by asking which was more of a concern to the respondent, the potential for vote fraud or the potential that eligible voters could be denied the right to vote? In response, 49% believed that vote fraud was more of a concern and 44% believed that denying eligible voters the right to vote was more of a concern.

These survey results suggest that the public's support for photo ID has remained steady over the past six years. That is, according to the polls examined for this report, a majority of the public believe that voters should show photo ID to vote, and a plurality believe that both vote fraud and vote suppression are major problems. When voters were asked in one poll to rank which was of greater concern—vote fraud or denying the right to vote—vote fraud ranked first by five percentage points and denying eligible voters ranked second.

Voter ID Legislation in the 112th Congress

Eight bills introduced in the 112th Congress include provisions that pertain to voter identification, including photo ID. Six bills would broaden the identification requirement in the Help America Vote Act or in identification requirements in the states. One would establish a federal requirement for a voter to provide photo identification to vote in a federal election, and one would require a driver's license applicant to clarify whether the state will serve as the applicant's residence for voting purposes. None have received committee or floor consideration.

Broadening the Identification Requirement

- H.R. 108 (Conyers) would amend the Help America Vote Act of 2002 (HAVA) to allow for the use of an affidavit to prove identity to meet the identification requirement in HAVA for voters who register by mail. It would also require the Election Assistance Commission to develop standards to verify information a voter must provide to register to vote in a federal election (a driver's license number or the last four digits of the voter's Social Security number). H.R. 3163 (Brown) would amend HAVA to prohibit an election official from requiring a state-issued identification to register or to vote in a federal election. H.R. 3316 (Ellison) would amend HAVA to prohibit a state or local election official from requiring a photo identification to register or to vote, either in person or by mail, in a federal election. It would also prohibit an election official from requiring an individual to cast a provisional ballot if the individual does not present a photo identification to vote. H.R. 3978 (Cleaver) would amend HAVA to require a state or local election official to accept a current, valid student photo identification from an institution of higher learning to vote in a federal election. H.R. 4126 (Cohen) would amend the National Voter Registration Act of 1993 (the "motor-

---

voter" law) to require states with a photo identification requirement for voting in a federal election to provide individuals who lack a government-issued identification with such an identification for free upon request. H.R. 6419 (Larsen) would amend HAVA to permit an individual to meet a photo identification requirement to vote in a federal election by signing an affidavit attesting to the individual's identification and that the individual is registered to vote.

Photo ID

- H.R. 6408 (Walsh) would amend HAVA to require an individual to provide a federal or state government-issued photo identification to vote, either in person or by absentee ballot, in a federal election. The requirement would not apply to military voters; the bill would authorize appropriations to cover state costs for providing free identifications to indigent individuals.

Clarify Residence for Voting Purposes

- H.R. 6386 (Miller) would amend the National Voter Registration Act of 1993 (the "motor-voter" law) to require an individual who applies for a driver's license to indicate whether the individual resides or resided in another state and whether the individual intends the new state to serve as the residence for voting purposes. It would require the motor vehicle authority to communicate such information to the individual's previous state of residence if the new state will be the voting residence.

Differences in Photo Identification Laws

As with many aspects of election administration, there is wide variation among the states with respect to verifying voter identity. According to the Government Accountability Office (GAO),[14] 31 states require a voter to show ID before voting at the polls on election day.[15] Of these 31 states with an ID requirement, some require a voter to provide *photo ID* in order to vote. Seventeen states and the District of Columbia do not require a voter to provide any identification document in order to vote, and Oregon and Washington conduct elections entirely by mail. In these two states, election officials mail ballots to all registered voters, who are not required to provide proof of identity when submitting the ballot.

Since the 2008 presidential election, 23 states have enacted 33 laws relating to voter identification, with 16 of them enacted in 2012.[16] For the 2012 election, 11 states will have a

---

[14] U.S. Government Accountability Office, *Elections: State Laws Addressing Voter Registration and Voting on or Before Election Day*, GAO-13-90R, October 4, 2012, p. 14.

[15] The exact number depends on how the laws are interpreted. For example, the National Conference of State Legislatures identifies 30 states with such requirements (see http://www.ncsl.org/legislatures-elections/elections/voter-id.aspx).

[16] According to the National Conference of State Legislatures (NCSL), the number of voter ID laws enacted by states in 2012 was the highest since 2003, when 25 were enacted in the wake of the Help America Vote Act's requirements (National Conference of State Legislatures, "Voter ID: State Requirements", 2012, at http://www.ncsl.org/legislatures-elections/elections/voter-id.aspx).

photo ID requirement in effect. An additional seven states enacted photo ID laws that have not yet taken effect or have been delayed from taking effect because of Justice Department or court action. A description of the photo ID requirements in the 18 states that have enacted such a requirement is shown in **Table 1** below. For each of the 18 states, the table presents information about the type of photo IDs accepted; the voting method used; exceptions to the photo ID requirement, if any; recourse if the voter is not able to comply with the photo ID requirement; and a comments column. The comments column has other information about the laws, including when the law was enacted, how it is administered, and exceptions that are permitted.

Some states accept a wide range of IDs, including ones that are issued by other states, while others limit the type of ID more narrowly. In Louisiana, for example, voters can meet the photo ID requirement with a driver's license or special ID issued by the state or "other generally recognized picture identification card with [your] name and signature."[17] The Office of Motor Vehicles will provide a free special ID card to any person who presents a voter information card. In comparison, Indiana voters must provide an ID issued by the state of Indiana or the federal government that includes a photo and a name that conforms[18] to the voter registration record and is current or that expired after the date of the last general election.

---

[17] Louisiana Secretary of State website, at http://www.sos.la.gov/tabid/457/Default.aspx.

[18] The name does not need to be identical to the registration record. Indiana Secretary of State website, at http://www.in.gov/sos/elections/2401.htm.

Table 1. Description of Requirements for States that Mandate a Photo ID for Voters

State	Type of Photo ID Accepted	Voting Method		Exceptions	Recourse if No ID	Comments
		In-Person	Absentee/ Mail-in			
In effect for elections in 2012 and before						
Florida	State DMV-issued Passport Military Student Debit or credit card Retirement center Neighborhood association Public assistance	X			Provisional ballot, counted if validated by signature matching.	
Georgia	State Federal Tribal Local govt. employee	X			Provisional ballot, counted if, *within 3 days after the election*, voter presents ID at county election office.	First enacted in 2003; amended in 2005 and 2006. State provides free ID. DL may be expired.
Hawaii	Not specified but must have the voter's signature	X			Voter must state date of birth and residence address.	ID must be provided upon request by a pollworker.
Idaho	State DMV-issued Federal Student Tribal	X			Voter must complete and sign affidavit, which must be accurate under penalty of law.	ID requirements enacted in 2010.
Indiana	State Federal	X		State-licensed care facility where the voter resides	Provisional ballot, counted if, *by noon of the Monday following the election*, voter presents ID at county election office or signs an affidavit declaring indigence or religious objection to being photographed.	ID requirements enacted in 2005, must include expiration date, which must be after the most recent general election.

State	Type of Photo ID Accepted	Voting Method		Exceptions	Recourse if No ID	Comments
		In-Person	Absentee/ Mail-in			
Louisiana	Generally recognized ID	X			Voter must sign affidavit and present other identification information required by election commissioners, and is subject to challenge.	
Michigan	Federal State (DL or ID card may be issued by any state) Student Tribal	X			Voter must sign affidavit.	ID requirements went into effect in 2007. ID must be current.
Went into effect for 2012 election						
Kansas	DL issued by any state State ID card Passport Government employee Military Student Government public assistance Government concealed-carry weapon license	X	X	Permanent physical disability preventing travel; absent active duty military and merchant marine and their families; religious objection to being photographed.	Provisional ballot, counted if, *before the meeting of the county board of canvassers*, voter presents ID to county election officer in person or by mail or electronic means.	ID may be expired if voter is 65 or older. Voters applying by mail for absentee ballots must provide either state DL or ID card numbers or copies of other accepted ID.
New Hampshire	*Before 8/30/2013:* Government-issued Student Other as determined by election officials (subject to challenge) *Thereafter:* State DMV-issued (any state) Passport Military	X		For registration, residents of care facilities may use a letter from the administrator rather than a photo ID.	Verification by election official (subject to challenge); voter-signed affidavit (subject to subsequent investigation for fraud),	Expired DL and passport may be used until 8/30/2013. Thereafter, date ID expired must be less than five years.

State	Type of Photo ID Accepted	Voting Method		Exceptions	Recourse if No ID	Comments
		In-Person	Absentee/ Mail-in			
South Dakota	State DMV-issued Federal Student Tribal	X	X		Voter must complete and sign affidavit, under penalty of perjury.	
Tennessee	State DMV-issued Any state-issued (in addition to TN) Passport Military	X		Indigence; religious objection to being photographed. Requires affidavit.	Provisional ballot, counted if, by the end of the second business day after the election, voter presents ID to county election officer.	
Enacted but not in effect in 2012						
Alabama	State Federal Government employee Student/employee (post-secondary school) Tribal	X	X		Regular ballot upon affidavit sworn by two election officials that attesting voter's identity and eligibility; provisional ballot, counted if, by 5 pm on the Friday after the election, voter presents ID at county election office.	Effective in 2014 if precleared by DOJ.
Mississippi	Government-issued	X	X	State-licensed care facility where the voter resides and votes.	Affidavit ballot, if, within five days following the election, voter presents ID at county election office.	Enacted by citizen initiative. Requires implementing legislation and preclearance.
Pennsylvania	Government-issued Student Care facility	X			Provisional ballot, counted if, *within 6 calendar days of the election*, voter presents ID and affirmation to county election office in person or via paper or electronic copy.	Implementation delayed until 2013 by state court. ID must include expiration date, except military; must be current, except state DL or nondriver ID may be up to 12 months past expiration date.
Rhode Island	State Federal Student (any state)	X			Provisional ballot, counted if validated by signature matching.	Effective in 2014. Specified nonphoto IDs are acceptable through 2013.

State	Type of Photo ID Accepted	Voting Method		Exceptions	Recourse if No ID	Comments
		In-Person	Absentee/ Mail-in			
South Carolina	State DMV-issued Passport Military State voter registration card	X			Provisional ballot, counted if, *before county certification of the election*, voter presents ID to county election office; or if voter completes an affidavit at the polling place attesting religious objection to being photographed, or a reasonable impediment to obtaining a photo ID.	Implementation delayed until 2013 by federal court.
Texas	State DMV-issued Passport Military Citizenship certificate Concealed-handgun license	X			Provisional ballot, counted if, *within six calendar days of the election*, voter presents ID to county election office ID or, under penalty of perjury, affidavit declaring religious objection to being photographed, or that lack of ID resulted from declared natural disaster within 45 days of casting of ballot.	Preclearance denied March 2012; decision upheld by federal court in August 2012. ID must include expiration date, except citizenship certificate; may be up to 60 days past expiration date.
Wisconsin	State DMV-issued Passport Military Student Tribal Certificate of naturalization	X			Provisional ballot, counted if, *by 4 pm on the Friday after the election*, voter presents ID to election office.	Ruled unconstitutional by state court in March 2012. Name on ID must conform to poll list; proof of residence required if not on ID.

Sources: Government Accountability Office, *Elections: State Laws Addressing Voter Registration and Voting on or Before Election Day*, GAO-13-90R, October 4, 2012, http://www.gao.gov/assets/650/649203.pdf; National Conference of State Legislatures, "Voter ID: State Requirements," 2012, at http://www.ncsl.org/legislatures-elections/elections/voter-id.aspx. Original statutory language was not checked by CRS in preparing this table to verify descriptions in the two sources, except to resolve conflicts or ambiguities between the descriptions.

Notes: Oklahoma has a photo ID requirement but permits use of a valid voter registration card in lieu of the photo ID. *DL* means driver's license. *DMV* means the state agency that issues drivers licenses. *Passport* means a U.S. passport. *State* means the state in which the voter is attempting to vote. States vary in whether *Student* IDs may be issued by high schools as well as postsecondary institutions, or whether they must be issued by a school in the state.

State rules also vary on what happens if a voter does not possess an approved photo ID. Of the 11 states with a photo ID requirement for the 2012 election, 7 (Florida, Hawaii, Idaho, Louisiana, Michigan, New Hampshire, and South Dakota) permit an individual to vote after signing an affidavit, by providing certain information to an election official, or both. The voter's eligibility may be challengeable or subject to subsequent investigation to verify eligibility. In the other four states (Georgia, Indiana, Kansas, and Tennessee), a voter who does not have the required photo ID may be eligible to cast a provisional ballot that will be counted if the voter provides an accepted ID after the election. A Louisiana voter must sign an affidavit and present other identification information (a utility bill, payroll check, or government document with the voter's name and address) to an election official, and may be subject to challenge. In contrast, an Indiana voter who lacks the required photo ID can cast a provisional ballot that will be counted if the voter appears at the county elections office by noon on the Monday after the election and either brings the required ID or signs an affidavit affirming indigence or religious objection to being photographed.

As noted above, some photo ID states strictly enforce the photo ID requirement—the voter cannot cast a regular ballot in person without providing a required ID—while others require a photo ID but will allow a voter without one to verify his or her identity by some other means. Georgia and Indiana were the first states to enact photo ID requirements in 2003 and 2005, respectively, and both strictly enforce the photo ID requirement. Georgia provides free photo ID to any voter and both states make allowances for voters with expired photo ID.

Most of the states that adopted a strict photo ID requirement have done so in the past two years. Kansas and Tennessee enacted strict photo ID laws that will be in effect for the first time in the 2012 election. An additional six states enacted strict photo ID laws in 2011 or 2012 that will *not* be in effect for the 2012 election because of court or DOJ action: Alabama, Mississippi, Pennsylvania, South Carolina, Texas, and Wisconsin. State activity on photo ID has raised various legal questions and issues, particularly with respect to the constitutionality of such laws and enforcement of the Voting Rights Act.

Legal and Constitutional Issues Regarding Voter Photo Identification Laws[19]

Photo Identification Laws and the Voting Rights Act

Whether voter photo ID laws comport with the Voting Rights Act (VRA) has recently been considered by the courts and the U.S. Department of Justice (DOJ). For example, in March 2012, DOJ denied preclearance approval under Section 5 of the VRA to laws in Texas and South Carolina that require voters to show photo ID prior to casting a ballot. Subsequently, as discussed below, federal courts also denied preclearance to both laws so they will not be in effect for the November 6, 2012, election. The South Carolina law, however, was granted preclearance to take effect in any election beginning in 2013. In addition, in July 2012, the department requested information from Pennsylvania in order to determine whether its voter photo ID law comports with Section 2 of the VRA.

---

[19] This portion of the report was written by L. Paige Whitaker, Legislative Attorney.

Section 5 of the Voting Rights Act

Section 5 of the VRA[20] requires certain covered states and jurisdictions with a history of voting discrimination to obtain preclearance approval before implementing a change to any voting practice or procedure. Covered jurisdictions have the option of seeking preclearance from either the U.S. Attorney General or the U.S. District Court for the District of Columbia. In order to be granted preclearance, covered jurisdictions have the burden of proving that a proposed voting change neither has the purpose, nor will have the effect, of denying or abridging the right to vote on account of race or color or membership in a language minority group. A proposed change will be determined to have a discriminatory effect—and accordingly, preclearance will be denied—if it will lead to retrogression in minority voting strength.

Covered jurisdictions are determined under a formula set out in Section 4(b) of the VRA.[21] Currently, nine states are covered: Alabama, Alaska, Arizona, Georgia, Louisiana, Mississippi, South Carolina, Texas, and Virginia. In addition, portions of seven other states are covered: California, Florida, Michigan, New Hampshire, New York, North Carolina, and South Dakota.[22] For further discussion of the VRA's preclearance requirements, see CRS Report R42482, *Congressional Redistricting and the Voting Rights Act: A Legal Overview*, by L. Paige Whitaker.

In March 2012, DOJ denied preclearance under Section 5 to a Texas voter photo ID law—also known as Senate Bill 14[23]—finding that the state did not meet its burden of showing that the law, as compared to the benchmark of existing law, will not have a retrogressive effect on minority voting strength. DOJ further determined that Texas failed to demonstrate why it could not achieve its stated goal of safeguarding election integrity in another manner that did not have a retrogressive effect.[24]

Texas filed suit in January 2012 seeking judicial preclearance under Section 5 for its voter photo ID law. Among other things, in this case Texas argued that its law resembles an Indiana voter photo ID law that was upheld on equal protection grounds by the Supreme Court in *Crawford v. Marion County Election Board*, discussed below, and a Georgia voter photo ID law that was granted preclearance in 2005. In the alternative, Texas challenged the constitutionality of Section 5. Trial in this case occurred in July 2012.

In August 2012, in *Texas v. Holder*,[25] a three-judge panel of the U.S. District Court for the District of Columbia denied preclearance to the Texas voter photo ID law. In a unanimous ruling, the court determined that the photo ID requirement will disproportionately impact African American and Hispanic voters, and is likely to lead to retrogression in minority voting strength. Specifically, the court found that Texas did not meet its burden of proving that its voter photo ID law will not have a retrogressive effect on minority voting strength. According to the court, uncontested evidence demonstrated that the "implicit costs" of obtaining the requisite photo ID in order to cast

---

[20] 42 U.S.C. §1973c.

[21] 42 U.S.C. §1973b.

[22] 28 C.F.R. pt. 51, app. (2011), "Jurisdictions Covered Under Section 4(b) of the Voting Rights Act, As Amended."

[23] Act of January 1, 2012, ch. 123, 2011 TEX. GEN. LAWS 123, codified at TEX. ELEC. CODE §63.001.

[24] *See* http://www.justice.gov/crt/about/vot/sec_5/pdfs/l_031212.pdf.

[25] 2012 U.S. Dist. LEXIS 127119 (D.D.C. Aug. 30, 2012).

a ballot will "fall most heavily on the poor and that a disproportionately high percentage of African Americans and Hispanics in Texas live in poverty."[26] Therefore, it denied preclearance.

The court was careful to underscore the narrowness of its opinion, however. Characterizing the Texas law as "the most stringent in the country," the court emphasized that its opinion should not be interpreted to suggest that preclearance could not be granted to other voter photo ID laws in other covered states where free photo ID could be easily obtained, and where documentation required to obtain ID was also free. Notably, the court did not reach the question of Section 5's constitutionality. With the consent of the parties, the court deferred consideration of the constitutional challenge to another phase of the litigation, and asked the parties to file a proposed schedule. Although the state of Texas has appealed the decision, there is insufficient time for the law to be approved and put into effect for the November 2012 election. As required by a provision of the VRA, any appeal of this case will be considered directly by the U.S. Supreme Court.[27]

Similarly, in December 2011, DOJ denied preclearance under Section 5 to a South Carolina voter photo ID law finding that the state did not meet its burden of showing that the law, as compared to the benchmark of existing law, will not have a retrogressive effect on minority voting strength. The Justice Department determined that non-white voters are significantly burdened by the law and disproportionately unlikely to have the requisite types of photo ID. In February 2012, the state of South Carolina appealed the Justice Department's denial of preclearance in federal district court. Among other arguments, South Carolina maintained that because the Supreme Court upheld a similar Indiana voter photo ID law, denying preclearance to the South Carolina law would raise "serious constitutional concerns" about whether Section 5 violates South Carolina's right to equal sovereignty, which should be avoided.

Following a September trial, on October 10, 2012, in *South Carolina v. Holder*,[28] the U.S. District Court for the District of Columbia decided not to grant preclearance to the law for the 2012 elections, but did preclear the law to take effect in any election beginning in 2013. As required by Section 5, the court compared the new law against the benchmark of the prior voter ID law. According to the court, like the prior law, the new law permits citizens with non-photo voter registration cards to vote without a photo ID, so long as they state the reason for not having obtained one. These voters are required to sign an affidavit stating the reason that they have not obtained a photo ID. In addition, as compared to the prior law, the court found that the new law expands the list of qualifying photo IDs that may be used to vote—adding passports, military IDs, and new photo voter registration cards—and makes it much easier to obtain a qualifying photo ID. Under the new law, photo voter registration cards may be obtained for free at each county's elections office and free photo ID cards are provided for at each county Department of Motor Vehicle (DMV) office, which under the prior law cost $5. Accordingly, the court concluded that the South Carolina law does not have a discriminatory retrogressive effect. The court also found that the new law was not enacted for a discriminatory purpose.

While granting preclearance to the law for any election beginning in 2013, the court found that there was insufficient time to implement the law for the November 6, 2012, election. According to the court, numerous steps need to be taken in order to implement the law properly and insure

---

[26] *Id.*

[27] 42 U.S.C. §1971(g).

[28] 2012 U.S. Dist. LEXIS 146187.

that it would not have a discriminatory retrogressive effect on African American voters, which cannot be accomplished in time for the 2012 election.

Section 2 of the Voting Rights Act

In contrast to Section 5, Section 2 of the VRA[29] applies to all jurisdictions in the United States. It provides a right of action for private citizens or the government to challenge discriminatory voting practices or procedures. Specifically, Section 2 prohibits any voting qualification or practice that results in the denial or abridgement of the right to vote based on race, color, or membership in a language minority. The statute further provides that a violation is established if, "based on the totality of circumstances, it is shown that the political processes leading to nomination or election in the State or political subdivision are not equally open to participation by [members of a racial or language minority group] in that its members have less opportunity than other members of the electorate to participate in the political processes and to elect representatives of their choice."[30]

In July 2012, the Department of Justice requested information from the chief election official of Pennsylvania in order to determine whether its voter photo ID law complies with Section 2 of the VRA. Among other information, the department requested Pennsylvania's current voter registration list, driver's license and personal identification list, and any documentation to support the governor's March 14, 2012, press release stating that 99% of Pennsylvania's eligible voters have the requisite photo ID.[31]

Constitutionality of Voter Photo ID Laws

The constitutionality of voter photo identification laws has also been considered by the courts. For example, there has recently been litigation regarding a Pennsylvania law requiring voters to show photo ID prior to casting a ballot. In 2008, the U.S. Supreme Court upheld a voter photo ID law under the U.S. Constitution on equal protection grounds. However, in more recent cases— including the litigation in Pennsylvania—the question being considered is whether voter photo ID laws violate relevant *state* constitutions.[32]

In *Crawford v. Marion County Election Board*,[33] the Supreme Court upheld an Indiana voter photo ID law against a facial challenge that it violates the Equal Protection Clause of the 14th Amendment to the U.S. Constitution. The Indiana law requires voters to present a photo identification card issued by the government.[34] In its 1966 decision, *Harper v. Virginia Board of*

---

[29] 42 U.S.C. §§1973, 1973b(f).

[30] 42 U.S.C. §1973(b).

[31] *See* http://images.politico.com/global/2012/07/dojpavoteridltr1.pdf.

[32] *See also, e.g.,* League of Women Voters of Wisconsin Education Network, Inc. v. Walker, No. 11 CV 4669, (Wis. March 12, 2012) (enjoining a Wisconsin voter photo ID law finding that its requirements are unconstitutional because they abridge the right to vote); Democratic Party of Georgia, Inc. v. Perdue, 288 Ga. 720, 707 S.E.2d 67 (2011) (upholding a Georgia voter photo ID law finding that it is authorized by the state constitution as a reasonable procedure for verifying voter identity and does not violate the state constitution as an impermissible qualification on voting because it does not disenfranchise voters).

[33] 553 U.S. 181 (2008).

[34] 2005 IND. ACTS 109, codified at IND. CODE §3-11-8-25.1.

Elections,[35] the Court determined that a state will be in violation of the Equal Protection Clause if it conditions the right to vote on the payment of a poll tax. According to the Court, making the affluence of a voter or payment of a fee an electoral standard is "invidious discrimination." This standard was later confirmed in *Anderson v. Celebrezze*,[36] where the Court said that *Harper* is satisfied by "evenhanded restrictions" that safeguard election integrity, and that a court must weigh the state interests justifying a voting restriction against the burdens it creates.

Although a majority of the Court in *Crawford* did not agree on a rationale for upholding the voter photo ID law, the lead opinion found that although the voter photo ID law imposes a "somewhat heavier burden" on a "limited number" of people, the severity of that burden is mitigated by the fact that eligible voters may cast provisional ballots that will ultimately be counted.[37] Moreover, even if the burden cannot be justified to a few voters, it would be insufficient to establish the relief sought by the petitioners in this case, which was to invalidate the voter photo ID law in all its applications. The lead opinion concluded that Indiana's voter photo ID law imposed only a "limited burden" on voting rights that are justified by the state interest in protecting election integrity.[38] Notably, the opinion pointed out that a nondiscriminatory law justified by neutral state interests should not be ignored merely "because partisan interests may have provided one motivation" for its enactment.[39] For further discussion of the *Crawford* decision, see CRS Report RS22882, *The Constitutionality of Requiring Photo Identification for Voting: An Analysis of Crawford v. Marion County Election Board*, by L. Paige Whitaker. For an analysis of First Amendment challenges to photo identification laws, see CRS Report R40515, *Legal Analysis of Religious Exemptions for Photo Identification Requirements*, by Cynthia Brougher.

In August 2012, a state court declined to enjoin a Pennsylvania voter photo ID law on the grounds that it violates the Pennsylvania Constitution. In *Applewhite v. Pennsylvania*,[40] the court rejected petitioners' arguments that the voter photo ID law violates the right to vote, which is expressly guaranteed by the Pennsylvania Constitution; imposes unequal burdens on the right to vote in violation of equal protection guarantees; and adds an additional qualification on the right to vote. Noting that the Supreme Court in Crawford had upheld the constitutionality of a similar Indiana law without evidence of in-person voter fraud, the court found that the absence of such evidence in this case was not dispositive. The court also referenced *Crawford* when it considered allegations of partisan motivation behind the Pennsylvania law, and determined that this evidence did not invalidate the governmental interests supporting the law. In conclusion, the court found that the voter photo ID law was a reasonable, non-discriminatory, and non-severe burden, and that Pennsylvania's interest in safeguarding public confidence in elections was "sufficiently weighty" to justify it. Additionally, the court said that it reached its decision employing the "federal 'flexible'" standard, and alternatively, the "substantial degree of deference/gross abuse" standard, but pointed out that if it had evaluated the law under strict scrutiny, it might have reached a different conclusion. Similar to the Supreme Court in *Crawford*, the Pennsylvania court observed that the remedy sought by petitioners—invalidating and enjoining the law in its entirety—was too

---

[35] 383 U.S. 663 (1966).

[36] 460 U.S. 780 (1983).

[37] *Id.* at 199.

[38] *Id.* at 203.

[39] *Id.* at 204.

[40] *See* No. 330 M.D. 2012, (Pa. Aug. 15, 2012), at http://www.pacourts.us/NR/rdonlyres/676A25C6-3760-4376-B7EF-71EA4A6623F9/0/CMW330MD2012ApplewhiteDetermPrelimInj_081512.pdf.

broad, and that a more reasonable remedy would be to challenge the law as applied to a few qualified electors on whom it imposes an enhanced burden.

This decision was appealed to the Supreme Court of Pennsylvania. In September 2012, the Pennsylvania Supreme Court vacated the lower court decision and returned the case to the lower court for further proceedings. Specifically, the court requested an assessment by the lower court of the availability of alternate identification cards, and stated that if the court determined that the voter photo ID law will result in voter disenfranchisement in the November 6, 2012, election, then it is obligated to issue a preliminary injunction.[41]

On October 2, 2012, the lower court issued a preliminary injunction to a portion of the law.[42] Among other findings, the court concluded that in the remaining five weeks before the general election, the gap between the number of photo IDs issued and the estimated need for IDs will not be closed, and therefore predicted that implementation of the law at the upcoming election would result in voter disenfranchisement. As a result, at the November 6 election, election officials in Pennsylvania will be permitted to ask voters for the requisite ID, but will be required to accept and count the ballots of qualified voters who do not present ID, and such voters will not be required to cast provisional ballots.

Implementation Issues and Policy Considerations

Election administration changes have the potential to introduce a degree of uncertainty in the voting process simply because they involve new procedures. This is especially true in the first election for which they are implemented. The administration of federal elections by state and local jurisdictions is a complex, interconnected process, in which steps taken to address potential problems at any point may have both expected and unexpected effects, not only on the problem being addressed, but on other parts of the process, and on individual voters as well. Implementing such changes may reduce the resources available for other tasks before the election, or may have unforeseen effects that would require correction. Some changes affect a limited number of voters, such as changing the location of an individual polling place or introducing new voting equipment in a jurisdiction, while others affect all the voters in the state, such as changing voter registration or identification procedures. In both cases, election officials may be required to educate the voting public about the changes and make the necessary adjustments to poll worker training and procedures before the election to insure a smooth transition on election day. Voters need to understand the changes and undertake actions to insure that they do not jeopardize their ability to cast a ballot.

It may be advantageous to have as much time as possible to implement changes to voting procedures, so that election officials, poll workers, and voters have time to adjust. The new photo ID procedures in effect for 2012 may provide a test of that view. There is no universal voting ID that is used in the United States (including the voter registration card, which is mostly used to provide information for the voter rather than for identification). Acceptable forms of identification differ by state and may be obtained from different agencies or entities within each

---

[41] *See* Applewhite v. Pennsylvania, 2012 Pa. LEXIS 2151 (Pa. Sept. 18, 2012).

[42] *See* Applewhite v. Pennsylvania, No. 330 M.D. 2012, (Pa. Oct. 2, 2012), at http://www.pacourts.us/NR/rdonlyres/CFBF4323-B964-4846-8179-88D689375C10/0/CMWSuppDetAppPrelInjOrder_100212.pdf.

state. Voters who possess one of the acceptable IDs need not take any action except to bring it with them to the polling place.

In states with strict ID requirements, voters who do not have an acceptable ID must secure one in order to cast a ballot. Sometimes the voter must obtain another document first, such as a birth certificate, as proof required for the voter ID.[43] It is also possible that a voter may possess an approved ID that does not match the information in the voter's registration record, for example because of a recent name change due to marriage or divorce, which would require the voter to rectify the discrepancy.

Other issues that could arise because of new photo ID laws concern the use of provisional ballots, the potential for long lines, and the possibility that poll workers could misapply the new rules. Voters who do not have an accepted ID may, in some cases, cast a provisional ballot (see **Table 1** for state-by-state details). In states that have a strict ID law, the voter will need to present required documentation at the county election office within a specified time period for the provisional ballot to be counted. Long lines may develop because of the higher turnout that occurs in presidential elections in combination with new check-in procedures that require each voter to present an ID. Voters who are unaware of the new requirement and those who do not have an acceptable ID and will need to execute an affidavit or vote a provisional ballot may cause delays and complications. Finally, there is the possibility that some poll workers will not be sufficiently trained to know which IDs are acceptable (particularly in states that accept a range of federal, state, and other IDs), which voters, if any, are exempt from the requirement,[44] and the procedures to be followed if a voter lacks the proper ID.

Whatever their individual views on photo ID or other voting requirements, most observers would probably agree on these two goals: (1) that all eligible voters should have equal opportunity to cast a ballot, and (2) that all necessary steps should be taken to protect the election process from fraud, abuse, and error at any stage. Both of those goals are arguably essential to ensuring the integrity of elections, but both are sometimes thought of as conflicting. It may be reasonable to suppose that the more focus is placed on providing access to the ballot box for all eligible voters, the greater the risk that people who do not meet the criteria for eligibility—for example by reason of non-citizenship, non-residence, criminal history—will be improperly included on the voter roles, or succeed in voting despite not being on the roles. It may also be reasonable to suppose that the more focus is placed on preventing fraud and abuse, the greater the risk that people who do meet the fundamental criteria for eligibility will be improperly excluded from the voter rolls, or not succeed in voting despite being on the rolls.[45]

It could be that the apparent conflict is in fact a false one—for example, changes to the election process aimed at increasing access or at decreasing fraud might not have significant effects on

---

[43] CBS News, "Pa. Law Hampers Some Voters From Getting IDs," September 28, 2012, at http://www.cbsnews.com/8301-18563_162-57521927/pa-law-hampers-some-voters-from-getting-ids/.

[44] In some states, indigent voters and those with a religious objection to being photographed are exempt from the photo ID requirement. For more information, see CRS Report R40515, *Legal Analysis of Religious Exemptions for Photo Identification Requirements*, by Cynthia Brougher.

[45] Some observers have proposed solutions that might reduce the risk of such a conflict, for example, by placing digital photographs of registered voters in electronic pollbooks, thereby eliminating the need for most voters to present separate identification documents (Caltech/MIT Voting Technology Project, *Voting: What Has Changed, What Hasn't, and What Needs Improvement*, October 18, 2012, at http://www.vote.caltech.edu/sites/default/files/Voting%20Technology%20Report_final.pdf).

---

actual access and fraud—or that the impact of any particular measure that seems likely to be effective is in fact minimal. No broad consensus has emerged on how to interpret the data that exist.[46] That uncertainty is not surprising, given both the complexities of the election process and the difficulties of collecting data about it that are amenable to scientific analysis.[47]

The lack of data may also explain the somewhat paradoxical views of election officials on voter photo ID. Two scientific surveys of local election officials in 2006 and 2008 found that on average they supported a photo ID requirement but believed it would have a negative effect on turnout. They also believed it would increase election security even though they found voter fraud uncommon and not a serious problem in their jurisdictions.[48]

A systematic approach to achieving the two goals discussed above would presumably include a risk analysis of all steps in the election process with respect to each goal. In recent elections, attention has shifted among different points in the process, with voter identification being subject to significant legislative attention in 2012. But in the absence of systematic risk analyses, it is difficult to determine what points in the election process—voter registration, voting systems, polling place location and hours, pollworker training, voter identification, vote tabulation, or other steps—actually involve the greatest potential risks to election integrity and therefore what priorities would be most effective for reducing those risks.

Concluding Observations

Given recent state legislative activity on photo ID and identification requirements generally, it is likely that legislators in the states will continue to consider similar legislation in 2013 and beyond. According to NCSL, 326 identification bills were considered in 41 states during legislative sessions in 2011 and 2012.[49] Further action in the courts and DOJ should be expected as well on photo ID as several new laws are slated to go into effect in 2013 or 2014 (Pennsylvania, Rhode Island, and South Carolina) or must be submitted for preclearance (Alabama and Mississippi). Finally, the 2012 election may provide useful data on the implementation and performance of photo ID laws, and Congress has routinely held post-election oversight hearings on the voting process in recent years. The impact of photo ID laws in a growing number of states is likely to continue to be a topic of high interest for the foreseeable future.

---

[46] See, for example, the disparate views presented in two recent books: Lorraine Carol Minnite, *The Myth of Voter Fraud* (Ithaca [N.Y.]: Cornell University Press, 2010); John Fund, *Who's Counting?: How Fraudsters and Bureaucrats Put Your Vote at Risk* (New York: Encounter Books, 2012).

[47] For example, one study found that more stringent voter ID requirements was associated with lower turnout, but the effect was small, there was no evidence of an effect of photo ID per se, and no evidence was presented with respect to impacts on voter fraud (The Eagleton Institute of Politics and The Moritz College of Law, *Best Practices to Improve Voter Identification Requirements* (Election Assistance Commission, June 28, 2006), at http://www.eac.gov/assets/1/workflow_staging/Page/62.PDF).

[48] CRS Report R41667, *How Local Election Officials View Election Reform: Results of Three National Surveys*, by Eric A. Fischer and Kevin J. Coleman.

[49] The NCSL 2011-2012 Elections Legislation Database, at http://www.ncsl.org/legislatures-elections/elections/2011-2012-elections-legislation-database.aspx.

Author Contact Information

Kevin J. Coleman
Analyst in Elections
kcoleman@crs.loc.gov, 7-7878

Eric A. Fischer
Senior Specialist in Science and Technology
efischer@crs.loc.gov, 7-7071

L. Paige Whitaker
Legislative Attorney
lwhitaker@crs.loc.gov, 7-5477

www.ingramcontent.com/pod-product-compliance
Lightning Source LLC
Chambersburg PA
CBHW080403290526
45790CB00009BA/3682